A Call
from the Shallows

poems by

Sunil Iyengar

Finishing Line Press
Georgetown, Kentucky

A Call
from the Shallows

Copyright © 2022 by Sunil Iyengar
ISBN 978-1-64662-849-0 First Edition
All rights reserved under International and Pan-American Copyright Conventions. No part of this book may be reproduced in any manner whatsoever without written permission from the publisher, except in the case of brief quotations embodied in critical articles and reviews.

ACKNOWLEDGMENTS

Poems in this book first appeared in some venues now defunct (*The New York Sun, American Arts Quarterly, The Rotary Dial*) and others happily among us still (*The New Criterion, River Styx, The Hopkins Review,* and *Literary Matters*).

Publisher: Leah Huete de Maines
Editor: Christen Kincaid
Cover Art: Andang Suhana
Author Photo: Kavita Iyengar
Cover Design: Elizabeth Maines McCleavy

Order online: www.finishinglinepress.com
also available on amazon.com

Author inquiries and mail orders:
Finishing Line Press
PO Box 1626
Georgetown, Kentucky 40324
USA

Table of Contents

I
Stepping Out, April 2020 1
The Living Room 2
Malvolio 3
Every Third Thought 4
Shore Leave 5
First Ride 7
To Catch a Thief 8

II
The Anti-Buddha 11
Change Agent 12
Hanuman's Mace 13
State Finals 15
Shipping Out 17
Petal Pool 18
One Hundred Days 19
How to Deal 20
Solace 21

III
The House across the Street 25
Not Helping 27
Singleminded 28
To Earth 29
Terminus 30
A Commuter's Vow 31
Backlit 32

I.

Stepping Out, April 2020

We roam like tropical denizens
down Rudyard, next street down from Hill.
The sidewalk's bare. Best avoid it until
floaters across your lens

are gone: a dog-walking pair,
a runner, and a gardener whose mask
is oddly suited to her bloodless task.
Dangling by the hair

a head of crab or clover,
she swivels on her haunches to make
eye-contact. Determined not to break
our stride, much less the cover

afforded by a scrim
of tall chestnuts, we keep to our side.
(There isn't any other place to hide.)
The runner passes, trim

and imposing, with a bow
as we prepare to fall behind
the two with their terrier. We've resigned
to take the sidewalk now

we're in the clear for once.
Though how much freedom do we hold,
who never ventured beyond a controlled
awe for certain house-fronts?

The Living Room

After the move we left things as they were.
Boxes in corners had not been unpacked.
Whole rooms existed merely as reminders
Of choice upon choice, steps we would defer
Until a day when, melting down our blinders,
The thought of live burial forced us to act.

Until that day, we almost were content
Outstretched in the living room, stretching out
The very definition of the place:
As if one room is where a life is spent,
Expanding to fill a preconceived space.
With no room to hide, there's no room for doubt.

And the day? It broke, most assuredly.
You left the room, started to poke around.
I heard cardboard rip, long belts of tape snap.
And though you were too far away to see,
The rug on which I lay exposed a gap
In what we had taken for common ground.

Malvolio

When I was born and you were not,
My parents hadn't found a name.
The birth certificate they brought
Home with me codifies their shame

As nurses saw them to the door,
Poor little things, and made them choose
A name right quick, but not before
They'd held a frank exchange of views.

("Try this one." "Too predictable."
"And that?" "You really want the kid
Ostracized?" "You don't think it's dull?
With all those *other* ones, you did.")

At last the couple trotted out
Reluctantly the name I bear
Today and which, never you doubt
It, child, pursues me everywhere.

A name most dictionaries ban,
A name to silence every room,
A name that since the world began
Must hide for laughter to resume

Its errand of assuring us
We come when called and will obey
An urge, however treacherous,
To lose ourselves along the way.

Every Third Thought

My friend, whose ruminations break
like surf against the rock that is
his forehead, constantly advises
others to learn from his mistake

and not dismiss as second-hand
articles washed up on the shore:
a Dunlop belt, a juice box, or
an undergarment filled with sand.

Anecdotes to be prized no less
than utterances chiefly sought
by lovers, children, and the lot
who hope that here will coalesce

in phrases no one else could want,
a piercing gull or, bound by murk,
on coral reef like lattice-work
the stray print of a cormorant.

As termites on a fallen birch,
still others comb the sand for lost
metal, accoutered with high-cost
equipment to perfect the search.

A sure sign of the amateur.
My friend agrees. He knows too well
to lust beyond a shoe or shell
is injudicious. Waves occur.

Shore Leave

Everyone's come to the beach for repose.
A slack interval
between bouts of immersion
in matters far away from here, and dear
only to others, to those
who can't or won't marvel
at skylines, at castles undone
or sculpted without fear
of cloud or ocean;
to those who must control

the view, applying the right pressure
on adversaries
much as a dark confessor
imprints the soul
it cleanses. Even like these,
scattered flecks of shale
report influences
not merely additive but
alchemical. The heat is gone
straight through, wilting a snail

or mollusk, whose armor for once is
eloquent: how life was squeezed out
and forced to lend its signature to stone.
Not so, our brave recumbents
here, sunning and semi-
exposed. If they should feel compelled
to quit their tents
or step outside the circumference
of skewed umbrellas
ever, it's only because

their gaze is minutely held
by a flash of sea
to which they now saunter.
Not that they would want to
accomplish or abandon
discipline at water's edge,
but rather for the privilege
of meeting a random
gesture with another kind:
to wage an ill-defined

campaign against the myriad
revolving schemes
that flatten out and gorge themselves on sand.
No one could have planned
it, how the bathers respond
to formlessness by forming into teams
oblivious of the bond
they share with one another and the land;
each traffics alone
in conceits of foam, arrogant and unwearied.

First Ride
> *in a supermarket lobby*

My name is Cinnamon Jack, the horse
children ride before they can walk.
My mane is as full as hair on a corpse
crowds of believers rend for a lock.

Cloth hooves joined to electric skis.
Handlebars riveted to my skull.
A whip for a tail, arrested knees,
and ears that would be laughable

did not they retain the warmth of fists
closed tight in panic or gradual trust.
Which one depends on whose mom insists
and whose dad favors might over must.

Still other hands proffer support
as each of you lunges in my dream.
To waist and shoulder they lend a sort
of benediction, proving extreme

tendencies can be moderated:
No matter how loud or fast my clip,
the whole experience is fated
to end before a loss of grip.

Ride on, newcomers. Ride until steps
start to be taken and lead you from here
to other diversions, knowing what depths
sustain a pendulum mid-career.

To Catch a Thief

My time is not my own, or mine alone.
Everyone says this. No one says it more
than those who have abundant time to spare.
They clearly fail to notice: what takes time
is patting down your pockets to make sure
you didn't leave it behind. "Tell me where
you might have seen it last." "Well, if I'd known
that," you retort, "I wouldn't have lost time

here in an alley, groping on all fours
under a street lamp just because it's bright
compared to someplace else I'd rather look."
Call time a fugitive: nothing sounds more trite—
unless you never willfully mistook
for theft a loss as intricate as yours.

II.

The Anti-Buddha

Luckless child, whose parents considered adoption
first, then yielded to frank necessity
under cover, the deed hardly fulfilling
but in that it threw off a covenant,
liberty of a kind. The problem came
soon after, when, beholding what they'd wrought,
father and mother took a vow right there:

They would not let blood-bias interfere
with how their son was raised, and how let go.
No sight was unworthy, no age too young
to launch his education. Frequently
a driver bore him past the palace gates
to scenes of destitution, blight, and death.
But none of it made any difference

to him. At last, steeped in the ordinary
modes of suffering, the way that other children
yawn in museums or shirk a piano lesson,
he grew to loathe these outings and escaped.
They found him under a peepal tree
in Gaya, sheltered as he'd never been
and preaching all he could about desire.

Change Agent

The parched road to the emblematic house
resigns to spitting gravel now and then
at visitors who wear their welcome out
by champing up and down it at full speed

while dandelions that raw fissures breed
are innocent of pairs who strolled here once
admiring as an oracle the house
whose tongue put forth a stranger in their midst.

A charismatic stranger, one who blurred
sentences in themselves impossible
to speak without rekindling arguments;
enveloped as a whole they sail on past.

The things that were got over! Little things
translated expertly so we could not
confer upon them further mystery—
so we might drown an artifact's laments.

We almost wish the mystery were not
susceptible to tampering. Never mind
the tourist-bus deposits made by day,
the hoary reminiscence cashed by night.

Inside, the gift shop permanence is real.
Ask children who insist on chocolate coins
minted in knowledge a bland profile will
retain its impression through gold tinfoil.

Hanuman's Mace

The worship they command is not the same
as in prior births, revealed to just a few
past monastery walls or temple doors.
Here everyone obtains an equal view:
stragglers from the Kingdom of Jade exhibit;
refugees from interminable tours,
perusing the alcoves for a place to sit;
and some who know each artifact by name

but wouldn't call these artifacts at all—
unless the term denoted what was made
sentient through yearning, a compact with stone.
They linger before idols once arrayed
in marigold and jasmine buds, where now
nothing remains but their wan monotone
features, portions of which have anyhow
eroded or been smashed without recall.

What tribute can they offer on the spot,
these accidental pilgrims, far from home?
The placard, if they read it, gives no clues.
"Iswara's phallus is worshipped as a dome..."
"Erotic touches such as these are common..."
The overall effect is to confuse
even the most ahistorical Brahmin,
who blinks at what interpreters have wrought.

A little farther on, the tools of trade.
A begging-bowl for alms, an incense-holder,
conches to summon prayer, a brass bell
shorn of tongue; then, a pole astride his shoulder,
a trunkless warrior bows as you take leave.
You won't be spared what every infidel
is only too accustomed to receive:
mute severance of that which will not fade—

sensory organs, limbs, an entire torso
obliterated; view the present case.
"Ninth-century Hanuman, shown saluting
Lord Rama. The stick likely bore a mace,
the weapon preferred by the monkey-god,"
as powerless to ward off serial looting
as you to rewrite captions that read odd
to some, to others ineffably more so.

State Finals
    Holiday Inn, Greenville, MS, 1982

Roped in, we file past spectators too scared
to wave or let a shutter blink, although
only one sound can shatter this tableau:
a word for which the tongue is unprepared.

The column ends at a microphone stand
propped on a platform, giving one the sense
of mastery unearned. In our defense
this march was not precisely what we planned

when plotting our campaign on friendly soil,
committing tracts to memory in case
by staring down the contours of a place
we'd know enough to not be judged disloyal.

Night after night the lists are fed to us
by those who say to conquer is to binge
and yet who cannot quite repress a twinge
of fear that what they do is dangerous.

Words were acquired wholesale, their meanings still
dark, as if asking were impertinent.
To pause to note the view from our ascent
was thought to be ill-timed or laughable.

Instead we learned to recognize the cut
of their apparel, consonant and vowel.
A kind of etiquette, to run afoul
of which could jeopardize our stepping out

onto a stage that traffics on occasion
high school reunions, coaching seminars,
wedding receptions, dancers and cash bars,
but never has upheld so many Asian

Americans. Here we are, joined in kind,
regardless of our provenance or past
vocabularies, lexicons amassed
elsewhere and long ago. We left behind

those badges of our own state sovereignty,
trading them in for ribbons we might snag
by pulling magic letters from a bag
each of us hugs as evidence of plenty.

And plenty we were promised, too. To blend
right in, provided we could win ourselves
distinction first: tin cups to line our shelves;
cast-out spell-books; a title to defend.

Shipping Out

The soldier in the park shudders
not for his fate, which remains
anonymous, like each blade of
grass that springs at his feet. No,
he cringes from the vapor trail
soaring above tenements
where 'park' claims all he has ever found
grand: cast-iron chairs, tables
where chessboards taught him strategy—
the benches where love's first blush
learned to burn in secret, to bide
its time, and once, by going under,
to make another burn right back…
Snapped-off branches give him pause.
Crows cut into the air, sideways.
And all the while he watches all:
each brown leaf he pocketed
restored to his own museum
of wishes, conquests, wonder.
And so tomorrow's flight, his first,
will dim as to nothing. He's gone
already, gone. The streetlights on
no more, suddenly, he gets up
and takes the park away with him.

Petal Pool

Roses in bloom, astonished at their own
brevity, throng the lip of the tall glass.
Petals divide, fall into the unknown,
kissing the tabletop before they pass
away, borne by air from a hidden duct
onto the floor, where they compose a mass
delegation, as if purposely plucked.

These exiles, while they dare not attract more
notice or praise than the roses themselves,
cast an impression too stark to ignore:
how no amount of tepid water salves
knowledge that a colony rests close by
whose members stand in for their better halves
and will receive them momentarily.

One Hundred Days
April 29, 2017

"The absence of a scar
Surely indicates
The shock's receding…"

"I wouldn't go that far.
No outer calm negates
Internal bleeding."

How to Deal

Luck is a neutral quality. You can't
wish it upon yourself or others, only
reminisce of the times you had it but
as yet were unaware. I don't say what
kind of luck, either good or bad. Don't count
on it beforehand. That way lies the lonely.

Nor will you want to flaunt your diffidence.
Luck has a way of letting one grow tense
whenever mention's made of never needing it.
So merely nod. Go on with your affairs.
Make eye contact if you must. By conceding it
a courtesy, nothing is lost. Or gained.
Just so, shrill piping on the lawn declares
a truce for moments after it has rained.

Solace

Storms descend on a late summer harvest.
The farmer left his plow inside a rut
The size of two upended skiffs, and hardest
Of woes, nobody helped him get it out.
Rains abuse it, gladly. The corn around it
Ripples in ecstasy. By mid-September,
Returning to wet fields, he will have found it
Transfigured to an altar. Howls dismember
Husks even as he takes the seat again,
Imagining a long unbroken wave
Retreats at his command. The darkest grain
Absolved at last, he preaches to the nave

Of an abandoned church, this barren plot,
Behold the lilies, just as he was taught.

III.

The House across the Street
for MDG

Six months ago a For Sale sign
sheltered against a fallen pine,
announcing the old Colonial free
of any claims to privacy.

It marked our chance, and by next week
most of our friends had had a peek
at what would have to be restored
for prices we could ill afford.

Wallpaper had been stripped, revealing
crust deposits from floor to ceiling.
Shag carpet more like undergrowth
hid allergies or ticks, or both.

The basement was unfinished in
the sense that it did not begin.
A torture rack or worker's bench
presided over wet dog stench.

The realtor in the kitchen stood
confirmed that we the neighborhood
upon the house had no design.
She stood, and waved, and sipped her wine.

So when we heard the place was sold
we pictured only walls of mold,
cigarette burns on worsted shag,
a basement from a horror mag

and could but think the fated tenants
ripe for self-inflicted penance.
So little did we know or guess
what deeds are brokered through largesse.

Provincial: isn't this the word
to signify that one has blurred
the contours of what can be done
so they seem scalable to none?

Circumscribed by what we'd seen
and not cut out to contravene
its original state of squalor,
we wore the floorplan like a collar

checking our curiosity
so that we might transmit pity
instead of loss, defeat, or shame
when time to meet the buyers came.

Not Helping

"We've never been close, really, so why start
Now?"—Thus a misanthrope declared when first
Advised of social distancing. "At worst
We're either six feet under or apart."

Singleminded

All our conversations have turned
abruptly, missing the distant prize
others have staked out and earned
by staying singleminded. One tries
instead to drink what another pours,
comment on the vintage, and to smile
until an empty glass assures
host and guest the talk was worthwhile.

"I'm not particular," you say
half-aloud in confidence
that any topic leading us astray
admits of its own thicket, dense
with ancestors and fellowships
only we can apprehend.
We coax them out with a few sips.
And there our divinations end.

While others can accept no less
than certainty at every turn,
a looming error to redress,
a new vernacular to learn,
we pride ourselves on seeing far
enough as needed—call it crass:
what are we *but* particular?—
to reach the bottom of the glass.

To Earth

I've chosen to meet you obliquely, to glance and dart
across your surface, attracting nicks and dings
so far, as yet no major wound. What of it?
There will be time enough to be steeped in you.

Terminus

Follow me into the dark. The mood here's
soft and indolent. Not what you'd expect
a cavern at the end of time to be.

No glaring revelation forces through.
You are left not with your own thoughts so much
as rinsed completely of them. Tourists wait

to snap the prize photo, and even you
for once are not concerned about bad hair.
The atrium fills with tepid conversation

on subjects for which one has ceased to care.
Distant drops admonish a standing pool
cool to the touch, if touch alone were possible
  and not this pause at every rock formation
  to wonder what it meant to you, and where.

A Commuter's Vow

By the time you get this, the train will have circled back.
Same conductor, same procession of cars, same smoke
and hissing. But peer inside lit windows and acquit me of
the return journey. I won't be there with the city folk
who shunt from home to work, who never reach above
their station. I'll switch, having shot out the wrong track.

By the time you get this, the statues will have shifted.
Same inscriptions, same pedestals, same verdigris flecked
with pigeonshit. But study their new postures for a clue
of revolt. I won't be towering among an elect
who bear the weight of children straining for a view.
Look hard. I'll push off before the fog has lifted.

By the time you get this, the scent will have gone cold.
Same flashlights and locked elbows, same hounds in pursuit.
Same photos on kiosks advertising French lessons,
nannies and summer rentals. All witnesses are mute,
but ask for me anyway. Try to recoup an essence
long gone into the grain with aspirations untold.

Backlit

My studio darkens. Last chance to pretend
  a few mote-troubled rivulets of light
catching on leaf clusters out there invite
  comparisons with sainthood. Branches bend
as if to nominate their choicest green,
  bedazzled and bestirred. As evening falls
on everything, a lost marauder calls
  it quits, atones behind a windowscreen.

As I atone, an insect or trapped bird.
  For not attending more to twigs as given—
sponsored by dark and light though little else.
  For not believing every leaf that whirred
held access to a contemplative heaven.
  For not renouncing mirror-worlds as false.

Sunil Iyengar lives near Washington, D.C., where he works as the research director for a federal cultural agency. His poems, book reviews, and essays have appeared in the *Los Angeles Review of Books, Washington Post, The American Scholar, The Hopkins Review, Literary Matters, Essays in Criticism, The New Criterion,* and other publications. He recently completed a novel in ottava rima—the verse form that Lord Byron used in *Don Juan*—and is editing an anthology of contemporary narrative poems. Iyengar was born in Barberton, Ohio, but moved around the United States as a child, graduating from the University of Michigan in Ann Arbor, then covering health policy and industry as a trade journalist. *A Call from the Shallows* is his first book.

www.ingramcontent.com/pod-product-compliance
Lightning Source LLC
LaVergne TN
LVHW040116080426
835507LV00041B/1186